5/10

Meet the Peacock

Suzanne Buckingham

PowerKiDS press.

New York

To my very colorful and talented writer friend, Lorijo Metz

Published in 2009 by The Rosen Publishing Group, Inc.
29 East 21st Street, New York, NY 10010

First Edition

Editor: Joanne Randolph
Book Design: Greg Tucker
Photo Researcher: Jessica Gerweck

Photo Credits: Cover photo, cover (logo), back cover, pp. 5, 6, 9, 10, 16, 19 Shutterstock.com; p. 12–13 © Stuart Westmorland/Getty Images; p. 15 © Martin Harvey/Peter Arnold, Inc.; p. 20 © Georgette Douwma/Getty Images.

Library of Congress Cataloging-in-Publication Data

Buckingham, Suzanne.
  Meet the peacock / Suzanne Buckingham. — 1st ed.
      p. cm. — (Scales and tails)
  ISBN 978-1-4042-4503-7 (library binding)
  1. Peafowl—Juvenile literature. I. Title.
  QL696.G27B83 2009
  598.6'258—dc22
                                                2008007743

Manufactured in the United States of America

Contents

Meet the Peacock

Have you ever seen a bird with a large fan of colorful feathers marching around the zoo? That beautiful bird is a peacock! Many zoos allow peacocks to walk freely around the grounds. This lets lots of visitors enjoy the birds' bright tail feathers.

Peacocks are the **male** birds of the peafowl family. The **females** are called peahens. Their babies are called peachicks. Peacocks and peahens both have crowns of feathers on their heads called **crests**, but peahens do not have long tail feathers, as do peacocks.

The peacock is best known for its beautiful, large, and colorful tail. The peacock generally opens its tail when it is trying to catch the eye of a female.

5

This is a blue peafowl. You can see the bright blue feathers on his neck, head, and crest.

Kinds of Peacocks

There are three different **species** of peacocks in the world. The blue peafowl has a bright blue neck and chest. This peacock is often found in zoos, but its natural home is South Asia.

The green peafowl has green feathers with black tips. It stands up straighter than the blue peafowl. Green peafowl are from Southeast Asia. In the wild they are an **endangered** species.

Congo peafowl live in Africa and were not discovered until the 1930s. The males are mostly dark blue. Congo peafowl do not have long, colorful tails, called trains, as blue and green peafowl do.

A Big, Beautiful Train

Peacocks are famous for their large, colorful trains. There are up to 175 feathers in a peacock's train. This train can grow up to 5 feet (1.5 m) in length. A peacock has short tail feathers behind its train. When the peacock wants to show off its train, these short tail feathers hold the train up like a fan.

Some types of peacocks have round spots on the ends of their train feathers. These spots are called eyespots. This is because they have dark centers that make them look like eyes.

A peacock's train feathers are not all the same length, so eyespots appear all over the train.

9

Here a blue peacock sits on a tree branch. With its heavy tail, it takes a lot of work for the peacock to fly!

Home, Sweet Home

Wild blue and green peafowl make their homes in the open forests of Asia. Congo peafowl live in the wet rain forests of Africa.

Peacocks spend most of their time walking around in small groups searching for food. After a tasty breakfast, peacocks **preen** their feathers before resting in the afternoon.

At night, peacocks roost on tree branches. Large groups gather and find tall trees where they can sleep close together. Peacocks sleep soundly on branches knowing they are safe from their enemies.

The Peacock

Tail Tales

- A peachick has a special tooth called an eggtooth that helps it break out of its eggshell.
- Adult peacocks weigh between 9 and 13 pounds (4–6 kg).
- Some peacocks can live up to 50 years. Most will live for about 20 years in the wild.
- A group of peacocks is called a pride or party.
- A peacock's colorful train is longer than its body.
- Peafowl eggs are light green or tan in color.
- The blue peacock is the national bird of India.
- Some peacock trains are made of all white feathers.
- A peahen picks which peacock she will have babies with by looking at his train. She usually picks the peacock with the most colorful and longest train.
- Peacocks can fly, but they usually make only short flights. Their large, heavy bodies make it hard to fly very far.

What Do Peacocks Eat?

Peacocks are **omnivores**. They eat both plants and animals. Peacocks usually move together in groups as they **forage** for food. They do not have any teeth, so peacocks swallow their pieces of food whole.

Peacocks enjoy leaves, berries, fruit, and certain parts of flowers. These hungry birds munch on **grains**, such as wheat, corn, and rice. Peacocks also dine on bugs. Some peacocks eat frogs, snakes, or other small **reptiles**. After a big feast, peacocks take a drink of cool water from a river, pond, or puddle.

This peacock is about to take a drink. He will then go back to looking for food with the other peafowl in his group.

Peahens, like these ones, have dull feathers and short tail feathers. This helps keep them safe from enemies.

Enemies of the Peacock

Peacocks have many enemies that hunt them, such as dogs, leopards, and tigers. With their long, colorful trains, these bright birds are easy to find. If a **predator** catches a peacock by his train, these long feathers usually fall out so the peacock can get away.

Peahens can fly away from enemies faster than peacocks. This is because peahens do not have long, heavy trains. A peahen's feathers are not bright like the peacock's. Her dull feathers **blend** in with leaves and bark. This helps her hide from enemies among trees and bushes.

A Peacock's Life Cycle

After mating with a peacock, a peahen lays about three to eight eggs. She keeps her eggs in a nest, which is a small hole in the ground lined with sticks. Peahens sit on their eggs to keep them warm. In 28 to 30 days, tiny peachicks begin to **hatch**.

Newborn peachicks can walk and feed themselves. A peachick grows a tiny crest after four weeks. At two months, a peachick is half its mother's size. Most peachicks leave their mothers at nine weeks. Peachicks become adults when they are three years old and then start new families of their own.

Peachicks have brownish feathers until they are older. Here one of the chicks practices fanning its tail feathers.

Peacocks like to talk to each other. This can make them interesting pets and noisy neighbors!

Proud and Loud!

You may think peacocks spend most of their time quietly showing off their wonderful trains. Guess again! These proud birds can be very loud! Peacocks and peahens have 11 different kinds of calls. They let out certain loud cries or honks to tell other peacocks an enemy is near.

Peacocks have a call they like to do early in the morning and late at night. This call sounds like, "May, awe, may, awe!" Peacocks and peahens also use special calls during mating season to find the right mate.

Peacocks and People

Peacocks are well liked for their colorful feathers, but peacocks can be useful, too. In India, wild blue peacocks eat lots of baby cobra snakes. These young snakes become a danger to people when they grow up.

People have kept peacocks as pets for thousands of years. Peacocks can live in warm and cold places, so they are found around the world. People in the United States, China, Europe, and other countries keep pet peacocks. Peacock owners do not seem to mind their pet's loud calls. They just enjoy watching their beautiful pets.

Glossary

blend (BLEND) To mix together completely.

crests (KRESTS) Head decorations on birds.

endangered (in-DAYN-jerd) In danger of no longer living.

females (FEE-maylz) Animals like women and girls.

forage (FOR-ij) To hunt or search for something.

grains (GRAYNZ) Small, hard seeds from food plants.

hatch (HACH) To come out of an egg.

male (MAYL) Animals like men and boys.

omnivores (OM-nih-vorz) Animals that eat both plants and animals.

predator (PREH-duh-ter) An animal that kills other animals for food.

preen (PREEN) To clean and oil feathers.

reptiles (REP-tylz) Cold-blooded animals with plates called scales.

species (SPEE-sheez) One kind of living thing.

Index

B
bird(s), 4, 12, 21
breakfast, 11

C
crest(s), 4, 18

F
fan, 4, 8
feathers, 4, 7–8, 11–12, 17, 22
females, 4

G
grains, 14
group(s), 11–12, 14

O
omnivores, 14

P
peachick(s), 4, 12, 18
predator, 17

R
reptiles, 14

S
species, 7

W
wild, 7, 12

Z
zoo(s), 4, 7

Web Sites

Due to the changing nature of Internet links, PowerKids Press has developed an online list of Web sites related to the subject of this book. This site is updated regularly. Please use this link to access the list:
www.powerkidslinks.com/scat/peacock/